PROJECTS

efore

I'M GOOD AT
MATHS
WHAT JOB CAN I GET?

Richard Spilsbury

WAYLAND

First published in 2011 by Wayland
Copyright Wayland 2011

Wayland
Hachette Children's Books
338 Euston Road
London NW1 3BH

Wayland Australia
Level 17/207 Kent Street,
Sydney, NSW 2000

Commissioning editor: Camilla Lloyd
Project editor: Kelly Davis
Designer: Tim Mayer, MayerMedia
Picture research: Richard Spilsbury/Amy Sparks
Proofreader and indexer: Alice Harman

Produced for Wayland by
White-Thomson Publishing Ltd
www.wtpub.co.uk
+44 (0)843 2087 460

British Library Cataloguing in Publication Data

Spilsbury, Richard, 1963-
I'm good at – what job can I get?.
Maths.
1. Mathematics–Vocational guidance–Juvenile
literature.
I. Title
510.2'3-dc22

ISBN: 978 0 7502 6574 4

Printed in China

Wayland is a division of Hachette Children's Books, an Hachette UK company
www.hachette.co.uk

Picture credits

1, Dreamstime/Hupeng; 3, Dreamstime/
Nruboc; 4, Dreamstime/Monkey Business
Images; 5, Shutterstock/Jorg Hackemann;
6, Dreamstime/Andreyuu; 7, Dreamstime/
Wavebreakmedia Ltd; 8, Dreamstime/
Imaginis49; 9, Dreamstime/Saladino; 10,
Dreamstime/Starush; 11, Shutterstock/
Dewayne Flowers; 12, Dreamstime/Micropix;
13, Dreamstime/Etherled; 14, Shutterstock/
Zoran Karapancev; 15, Dreamstime/Nruboc;
16, Dreamstime/Hupeng; 17, Dreamstime/
Chaoss; 18, Dreamstime/Tdmartin; 19,
Dreamstime/Jcpjr; 20, Shutterstock/
Lorelyn Medina; 21, Dreamstime/Mcpics; 22
Dreamstime/Lighthunter; 23, Dreamstime/
Shutter1970; 24, Dreamstime/Sviridow; 25,
Shutterstock/StockLite; 26, Dreamstime/
Jingaiping; 27, Dreamstime/Lindenblade;
28, Dreamstime/Monkey Business Images;
29, Shutterstock/Kailash K Soni; cover (top
left), Shutterstock/StockLite; cover (top right),
Shutterstock/Monkey Business Images; cover
(bottom), Dreamstime/Hupeng.

CONTENTS

The world of maths

What were the first maths skills that you learned? Counting fingers or toys, sorting things by shape, predicting what would happen next? Mathematics gives people powerfully simple ways to describe, analyse and change the world around them. It is a universal language. Most countries use exactly the same ways of writing maths and the same mathematical principles. People use maths every day to do all sorts of things, from counting money to measuring things and managing time.

↑ Vets need maths skills to assess changes in an animal's health over time, and to calculate safe and effective drug doses.

World-changing

Maths has transformed the world many times through the ages. Mathematicians first built computers to help do sums. Now we have computers in our homes, schools, offices and cars. Search engines such as Google use mathematical principles to rapidly search global data for information on the Internet.

Accurate weather forecasting enables people such as fishermen, builders, farmers and sports organisers to make decisions about when weather conditions will allow them to work outside. Forecasting relies on mathematical skills in assessing past weather data to make predictions about future weather.

If designers do not get their maths right, BMX riders might risk injury on unsafe ramps at parks.

Maths in the workplace

Workers in nearly every profession, not only bankers and engineers, need maths skills. For example, bakers need maths skills to weigh out the right ingredients for batches of loaves or cakes. Skate-park designers use maths to work out the right angles for slopes and curves of half-pipes to make sure riders can get up enough speed, land safely and have fun, while also building the park on time and within budget.

Special skills

If you are good at maths you will probably be good at a whole range of skills that could be very useful in future jobs. You will be able to think clearly and logically – approaching a problem step-by-step to find a solution. You will be able to organise information into smaller, more manageable chunks. If you study maths later, at college or university, you will develop these skills even further. These special skills are transferable to many jobs – this book introduces just a few of them.

Banker

Bankers help look after people's money and make money for banks. When individuals or businesses save their money in banks and building societies, they get small extra amounts called interest. Bankers create the interest by lending customers' money to individuals, for example to buy expensive houses that would take too long to save up for. Banks also lend money, sometimes at high interest rates, to businesses that want to expand. Banks make money when the interest they give customers on their savings is less than the interest they are making on the loans the businesses are paying back.

Job description

Bankers:
• often start work as juniors
• might work at a counter, taking in or paying out money, or advising customers about different types of savings accounts
• with experience and training, may become managers
• as managers, may have different duties, such as running a whole branch of the bank or coaching junior bankers.

City traders use their maths skills to understand financial data about businesses, in order to make money for banks.

What skills do I need?

Bankers will usually have studied maths, ICT and business at school. Many start work after A-levels, but some get a university degree. Finance and business courses have the greatest relevance. Banking involves meeting people and calculating, understanding or explaining financial matters, so good IT and communication skills are essential.

Different types of banker

Retail bankers work in high-street banks and building societies, serving individuals who come into branches or Internet customers. Commercial bankers deal with businesses, large or small. Investment bankers advise people about how much money they can borrow and how much interest they might have to pay.

City traders, or stockbrokers, are the gamblers of the banking world, who work at stock markets. These are places where small portions of the value of businesses, called shares, are bought and sold. Traders try to buy shares just before they rise in value, which happens, for example, when a business such as Apple brings out a new, successful product. They then try to sell before the share values fall, in order to make money for banks.

PROFESSIONAL VIEWPOINT

'My job relies on building and maintaining good relationships with my clients. It's vital that I understand what they want to achieve, and continue to deliver products, ideas and services that meet their needs.'

Sian, banker

Buying a home would be impossible for most people without a loan organised by a banker.

Cryptographer

Are you fascinated by codes and finding ways to break them? If so, you may enjoy using your mathematical skills to become a cryptographer. Cryptographers make and break secret codes for a living.

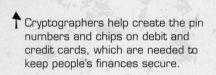

↑ Cryptographers help create the pin numbers and chips on debit and credit cards, which are needed to keep people's finances secure.

Lots of different businesses and organisations need cryptographers to keep information secret. For example, cable or satellite TV companies (including Sky) encode their signals so only viewers renting their decoding devices can turn the signals back into TV programmes. Banks encode data to make sure that financial information, ranging from what is in a bank account to the PIN number someone needs to use an ATM card, remains private.

What skills do I need?

Most cryptographers study maths and ICT at school. It is really useful to practise using codes. For example, learning a musical instrument helps you read musical symbols, which are a kind of code. You can read up on how codes were used in the past. For example, codes were vital in World War II to stop the Germans finding out about British military plans. Most cryptographers have a maths degree, but it's also important to have great patience and an interest in solving problems.

In antivirus software, cryptography is used to prevent hacking, phishing and other ways of gaining unauthorised access to your computer. The passwords you use on Internet sites and the security of online shopping all rely on the skills of cryptographers. Without them, thieves would be able to access your data and money.

↓ Satellite dishes on buildings around the world allow people access to lots of free TV channels, but TV companies encrypt some programmes so that only those who pay can watch them.

PROFESSIONAL VIEWPOINT

'Cryptography is a way of thinking ... it requires a certain kind of mentality to approach systems from an attacker's perspective. I find that good security people are games players and tinkerers. The ability to find loopholes in a system ... is vital to a cryptographer.'
Bruce, cryptographer

Accountant

Would you have the patience to check pages of numbers for mistakes? It sounds a bit boring, but it's an important job. Accountants check the financial records (or accounts) of individuals and organisations.

↑ Accountants often use calculators to help add up financial data and work out how much tax is owed.

PROFESSIONAL VIEWPOINT

'I don't think anyone grows up wanting to be an accountant. I always wanted to be James Bond. I've since learned that the majority of directors of large companies are chartered accountants, so that's the real benchmark for me ... I knew accountancy would provide me with an opportunity to move into almost any industry or commercial sector I like.'

Ross, accountant

Job description

Accountants:
- prepare and monitor financial records
- work out whether people are paying their fair share of taxes
- may work for just one company or for different businesses, either being employed by an accounting firm or as a freelancer.

Financial records can show, for example, whether or not businesses are making money. Checking accounts is also important because people pay tax to governments, based on how much they earn. Taxes are used to pay for schools, police, hospitals, roads and other things everyone needs.

Different types of accountant

The usual starting role is as an accounting technician. Technicians help prepare accounts and monitor company expenses. For example, if a company pays too much for office equipment, it may not have enough to pay staff. With qualifications, technicians can become chartered accountants, specialise in different areas (such as taxes or small businesses) and generally earn more than accounting technicians. Accountancy qualifications are recognised globally, so accountants may work in different countries.

↑ Accountants have skills that are needed by businesses and organisations all over the world.

What skills do I need?

Accountants need good detective skills and patience to piece together complete financial records from different sources. You will also need to be able to handle numbers confidently. Most accountants take at least A-level maths and sometimes a degree in maths or accounting. They might also do a business studies course to see how businesses work. It takes about three years to become a chartered accountant because of all the exams you need to take, through organisations such as the Association of Chartered Certified Accountants (ACCA). However, exams can be taken while you are already working as an accounting technician.

Economist

The economy means the way people and businesses buy, sell and distribute goods and services. Economists specialise in the study of how businesses, regions or nations are affected by and influence the economy. They examine the impacts of various factors by asking questions such as 'how much less do people spend when banks charge more interest on loans?' or 'are there fewer jobs when the government increases business taxes?'

↑ Economists need excellent presentation skills to explain their forecasts about the economy and to persuade others to make their recommended changes.

Job description

Economists:

- look at data to work out how certain changes affected the economy in the past
- use these results to predict the impact of future changes
- use mathematical equations and models, specialist software and research to make predictions or forecasts
- present their findings to others, and make recommendations for improvements.

PROFESSIONAL VIEWPOINT

'It's very satisfying to know that there's a direct link between what I do and what happens at the top levels of government.'

Imran, assistant government economist

Different types of economist

Some economists work for large organisations such as international banks. These banks sometimes lend money to countries for expensive projects such as building road systems. Economists in the banks might examine how the roads would improve transport and industries in a country, and therefore how quickly the country might repay its loan.

Other economists work for governments. Government economists might work on projects such as the impact of hosting the Olympics on a country's tourism, or how the international price of oil will affect the cost of food. Economists sometimes work for global businesses. For example, a company such as Ford may employ economists to work out the price people might pay for an exciting new car that they are developing. Then the company has to make sure that factories can produce it cheaply enough to make a profit.

What skills do I need?

Economists need confidence and an ability to cope with pressure, as they often have to make forecasts that could have a big impact on spending. Specialist skills and a broad understanding of local, national and international economies is important, so most economists have at least an economics degree. At school, it's useful to study subjects such as maths, business, politics, history and law.

Economists worked out the likely financial and social impacts of the 2008 Summer Olympics in Beijing long before the exciting opening ceremony.

Finance officer

Finance officers look after the finances of businesses or organisations. They combine some of the skills of accountants, bankers and economists. Finance officers often work with teams of more junior staff, and may report to a finance manager, depending on the size of the organisation.

Some finance officers working for charities may collect and count funds raised by big events such as city marathons.

Job description

Finance officers:

- prepare accounts for accountants to check
- make sure staff salaries are paid correctly and on time
- keep an eye on the spending in different departments
- keep up to date with any changes in laws, such as having to provide disabled access or fire training for all employees.

Different types of finance officer

Finance officers may work for local councils, charities, schools or colleges. A council finance officer controls the council budget. They have to check that the council can afford to run services such as libraries, waste collection and public toilets, using money collected through local taxes. In charities, finance officers keep track of donations (gifts) from the public, salaries for staff and payments to people in need.

What skills do I need?

Finance officers often start out as accounting technicians (see pages 10–11). They may spend five or more years at this level before building up enough experience to become an officer or finance manager. Finance officers are financial all-rounders, so it helps to work in different organisations. It's also useful if you enjoy working in teams and you are good at doing things on time. There are often important deadlines, such as dates by which grant applications need to be sent in.

A school finance officer (sometimes called a bursar) helps source and purchase services and goods in the school, and may check their quality. For example, if the school needs a new assembly hall, the bursar finds out how much the school can afford to spend, whether there are grants available to help pay for the hall, and checks the work of builders who construct the hall.

PROFESSIONAL VIEWPOINT

'People in my organisation may not get excited at the thought of my daily duties. But they do realise that the great work we do in educating students and remaining a cutting-edge college would not be possible without strong financial management.'

Amy, college bursar

Bursars may work closely with engineers to keep an eye on the costs of new buildings for their organisations.

Computer programmer

Computer programmers are expert in designing the code sequences that make computer programs work. Programmers are also known as software designers, developers or analyst programmers.

Different types of computer programmer

Some computer programmers are games developers, creating exciting games for computers and games consoles, such as Wii or Xbox. Applications programmers work on business applications. For example, some create programs that control how efficiently car engines use fuel. Some create search engines, such as Google, that many of us use to navigate the Internet.

PROFESSIONAL VIEWPOINT

'Just as it can be very frustrating, programming can be a very satisfying job. Solving a problem that has caused chaos and misery to a business is very gratifying. Writing code is often good fun and in many ways a creative process – it's YOUR program and you can write it how you like, as long as it does the job.'

Leon, applications programmer

↓ Some computer programmers work in different industries to automate production of goods ranging from cars to microchips using robots.

Applications programmers also make robots work. Industrial robots are programmed to carry out routine tasks such as painting cars or dangerous tasks such as handling hot, melted metal. Other more experimental robots are programmed to 'learn' artificially while carrying out tasks so they gradually improve their performance. Programmers also develop familiar products used in different industries. For example, the Hawk-Eye computer system is a program widely used in sports to predict from video film the exact direction and path of fast-moving balls. It is used to help players and referees confirm whether balls are in or out or on target.

Job description

Computer programmers:
- design computer programs using code
- change the code to generate reports about how programs are working
- fix problems
- enhance programs.

Computer programmers ➔ spend a lot of time in front of computer screens, writing and checking their software coding.

What skills do I need?

To be a programmer, good A-levels in maths, physics and ICT are very useful, and many programmers also have ICT degrees. Through these you will develop logical thinking. Your daily work will involve creating and following step-by-step instructions written in code. This is time-consuming and demands patience and accuracy. You sometimes need to think around problems to come up with better solutions. Fluency in a programming language such as C++ will be helpful. Although most companies will offer training, why not try to learn a programming language beforehand? Using the right symbols is vital when using code, so remember your punctuation!

Actuary

Do you get a buzz from playing games where winning depends on the risks you take? Then you might like to become an actuary. Actuaries work out the financial impact of risk for different businesses, including insurance companies, companies selling pensions, and banks.

PROFESSIONAL VIEWPOINT

'You have to try to work out why you're getting the results you're getting. You have to enjoy problem-solving. That's what appeals to me, using maths in a way that means something in the business sense.'

Katy, actuary

Electoral voters, shown here in voting booths, can vote for a change of government, which may affect a country's policies on pensions and health. Actuaries need to take such changes into account when calculating risk for pension companies, insurers and other clients.

Businesses often need to work out financial risks. For example, insurance companies offer cheap holiday insurance to people going on a beach holiday, assuming that not many of them will lose their luggage or have accidents. Insurance costs more for people going skiing or climbing mountains because these are riskier activities and there is a greater chance the insurance company will have to pay out money.

When actuaries are experienced enough to give expert advice, they need the ability to communicate their forecasts to non-experts. Practising public speaking at school will give you a head start. The wrong forecasts can be very costly, so actuaries need to understand how changes in laws, the economy and population trends will affect their data. For example, if a country will have a large proportion of older people in future, pension companies will have to pay out more money. This will affect how much they charge people for the pension plans they buy today.

In their work for insurance companies, actuaries work out the likelihood of natural disasters, such as hurricanes, occurring in different parts of the world.

What skills do I need?

Actuaries need good maths and computing skills to handle complex statistical software. Many study applied maths, economics or actuarial studies at college. These subjects help develop innovative thinking and problem-solving skills. You will need at least three years' experience in a job using actuarial techniques, such as in an insurance company, before you can take the professional exams. Some companies help out with the cost of the exams.

Medical statistician

Medical statisticians are a bit like health detectives. They search for data and statistics about people's health. They then analyse these to uncover links between health and lifestyle or taking certain medicines. Their work helps doctors, governments and drug companies answer questions such as 'Does smoking cause lung cancer?' or 'Does my company's heart drug work better than my competitor's heart drug?'.

Job description

Medical statisticians:

- create experiments to study the impacts of different things on the health of groups of people
- efficiently gather specific data required by the experiments
- write clear reports and effectively present data and conclusions to other people
- work as part of a team.

Healthcare workers, including doctors, routinely gather lots of data about patients. The data may include their height and weight, whether they smoke, the results of blood tests, and their general health. Like all statisticians, medical statisticians must decide what type of data to use, from all those available to them, and whether they need to collect more data to draw conclusions.

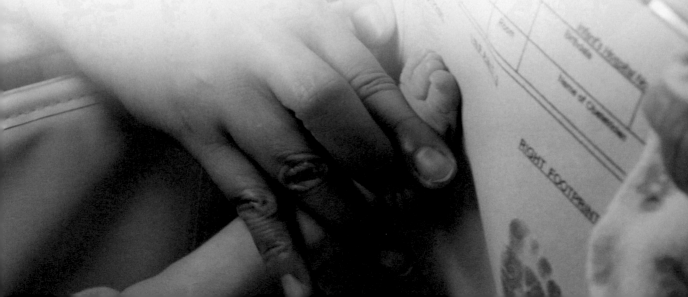

The basic statistics that medical statisticians use in their work are health data, some of which are taken by governments from the day we are born.

Different types of medical statistician

Medical statisticians (sometimes called medical researchers) work in different places around the world. Some work for university medical schools or international agencies representing many governments, such as the World Health Organisation. Others might work for private drug companies.

There are different types of medical statisticians. Epidemiologists work on the distribution and causes of disease. For example, they investigate air pollution across a city, region or country and find out whether more people get asthma in places where the air is most polluted.

Pharmaceutical statisticians examine data to find out how well medicines work. Drug companies need the statistical evidence they provide – that products work and are safe to use – before they start selling them.

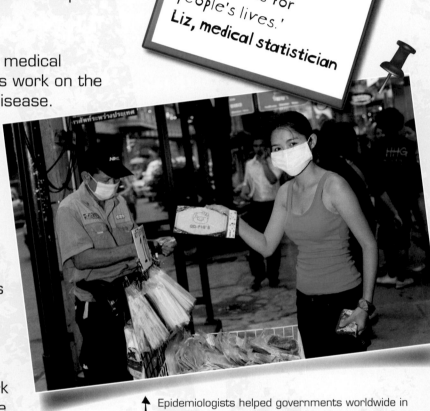

Epidemiologists helped governments worldwide in stopping the spread of Avian Flu, for example by recommending that people wear masks to avoid breathing in the virus.

What skills do I need?

Medical statisticians will usually have studied maths and science subjects at school. Most have a university degree, which can be in any subject although applied maths is especially useful. An interest in and understanding of medicine or biology is very useful, but being able to apply mathematical skills to these areas is more important.

Government research analyst

Running a country is a very complex job for any government. There are different departments looking after different specialties, such as schools or prisons. These departments need to prove they are spending money efficiently when offering public services. Government research analysts help governments make better decisions about what to spend money on, in order to deliver good services.

Government research analysts may → specialise in particular areas, such as evaluating whether different approaches to caring for the elderly offer value for money.

Job description

Research analysts:

- are sometimes called operational researchers
- usually work on a range of projects
- collect and interpret changing data on many issues in order to convert real-life complex systems or management problems into mathematical models
- draw conclusions that provide number-based evidence to support changes in government policies.

Different types of research analyst

Government research analysts work with many different government departments. For example, some work with the police and the Highways Agency to work out the best arrangement of speed cameras. Speed cameras cost money to set up and to monitor, so it makes sense to put them on roads where speeding is common, or where there are lots of accidents.

Other research analysts work for the Ministry of Justice to forecast the future demand for prison places, based on past and current rates of crime. This information enables the government to decide whether to build more prisons or employ more police to prevent crime.

What skills do I need?

Do you like to play chess, learn languages, or make science projects? If so, you probably have analytical skills – the ability to see and solve problems, based on what you know. These skills are vital for research analysts. Many analysts have very good degrees in maths or sciences, which require analytical skills. Like many government workers, research analysts work at different grades, with different responsibilities and salaries. Most start as junior analysts and build up work experience until they can lead teams and manage others.

Globally, road traffic accidents are the third most important cause of poor health. Analysts' work in positioning speed cameras can help slow down drivers and save lives.

Engineer

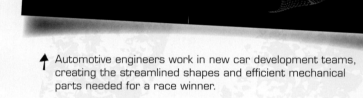

Every man-made thing around you has been engineered in some way, from a chair strong enough to sit on each day or an easy-to-use pen to a skyscraper or aeroplane.

Different types of engineer

↑ Automotive engineers work in new car development teams, creating the streamlined shapes and efficient mechanical parts needed for a race winner.

There is a wide variety of specialist engineers. Civil or structural engineers plan, design and construct buildings and infrastructure such as roads, bridges and reservoirs. These need to be able to withstand heavy weights and other stresses, such as ground movements or high winds, to meet human needs.

Aerospace engineers specialise in designing, building and operating flying machines, ranging from aircraft and helicopters to spacecraft, missiles and rockets. Mechanical engineers work on engines and other mechanical devices. Engineer roles change according to the needs of society. For example, in recent years environmental and sustainability – or 'green' – engineering has developed because people today want to make structures that have a less harmful impact on the Earth than in the past.

Job description

Engineers:
- use maths and scientific principles to invent, design and build things
- take on changing roles according to specialism and demand
- routinely work with other people on projects.

What skills do I need?

People who become engineers generally enjoy solving problems. At school and university, they are more likely to be interested in applied maths – using trigonometry (measuring angles) and calculating areas and volumes to solve real-life problems – than pure maths, although both sorts of maths are useful. Most also study a range of sciences at school and usually go on to do engineering or maths degrees. While they must enjoy working in a team, they also have to think independently to make sure that they find the best solutions to problems, rather than following the crowd. Many future engineers take part in science fairs, model-making clubs and design competitions at school.

↓ Structural engineers use their maths skills to help construct safe, stable and strong buildings and other structures.

Business analyst

Where will our customers want to go on holiday next year? Why are we selling more but making less profit? Businesses often employ business analysts to help them answer such questions. This type of information enables businesses to hold on to existing customers and get new ones.

↑ The profitability of a logistics centre, such as this one in China, relies on storing goods for as short a time as possible and delivering them speedily to different places. Business analysts can help make this happen.

Different types of business analyst

Business analysts are sometimes called operational researchers, like government research analysts (see pages 22–23). They work in many different industries. For example, in the transport or logistics industry, business analysts may work out the best ways to deliver goods cheaply and on time from central warehouses, while keeping the number of vehicles and amount of fuel used to a minimum. They work for well-known companies such as AOL, for example using feedback from customers to improve their websites to increase sales.

PROFESSIONAL VIEWPOINT

'Being able to translate business situations and problems into a mathematical model is an invaluable skill to possess in the corporate world. However, the full mathematical contribution can be achieved only by using "people" skills to obtain a clear understanding of the problem from the customer and then to interpret the "numbers" solution.'

Mark, business analyst

Job description

Business analysts:

- use their skills to improve businesses
- use past data and current data to predict people's future spending patterns
- make recommendations to businesses based on these data that will help them maximise income and retain customers.

Business analysts for tourism companies examine changing travelling patterns. They work out when people are likely to want to travel, where and how. They assess whether holiday destinations can meet demand from holidaymakers, and what price holidays should cost. Then they can offer holidays that customers want to buy, and make sure the same customers will travel with them again in future.

↓ Business analysts assist airlines to plan flight timetables so their planes are full of passengers and their runways are busy.

What skills do I need?

A-levels in maths, statistics and ICT will help you to analyse data and draw conclusions. Business analysts often have degrees, but some take BTECs in business or statistics and build up analytical skills while working for different businesses. Business analysts really need to communicate well because they often have in-depth discussions with different people in an organisation in order to gather and understand information relating to their work.

Maths teacher

Maths teachers or tutors set problems using different equations and give you sums to finish for homework. The chances are that you find these tasks pretty easy if you are reading this book!

Different types of maths teacher

Maths teachers work not only in primary and secondary schools, but also in further education colleges and universities, and from home as private tutors. Some specialise in teaching children of particular ages, while others teach maths to adults.

PROFESSIONAL VIEWPOINT

'Maths is the language underlying all of engineering and science. It's very rewarding to teach such a useful and universal language.'

Mark, business analyst

A good maths teacher can pass on maths skills to many individual learners of different ages and abilities.

Job description

Maths teachers:

- pass on the maths skills people need
- usually work from a curriculum, which is a written scheme of the necessary skills, often based on government requirements
- meet other teachers in a school or college to agree on how best to teach the curriculum to students of different abilities
- make sure maths departments have the right resources, such as books and calculators
- organise open days and competitions to showcase maths skills
- liaise with parents over homework and targets for students.

What skills do I need?

Being good at maths is not enough on its own. You must also enjoy explaining maths concepts to others. This can take great patience because some students are not keen on learning and others need to be taught in many different ways before information sinks in. It also requires creativity and communication skills. Maths teachers take teaching qualifications after studying maths or science subjects at college or after working in business. Maths teaching skills are transferable. Some teachers become tutors and others volunteer for charities, working overseas in less developed countries where there is a shortage of maths teachers.

Adult numeracy teachers may help people in particular trades with maths that will make their jobs easier. For example, electricians may need algebra skills to work out which electrical components are safe to use in a circuit.

At universities, maths lecturers usually combine teaching students and marking exams with research. They study complex maths problems and solutions, publish articles about their research, and attend maths conferences.

↓ Maths teaching skills can be put to good use in less developed parts of the world, as in this school in India. A lack of classroom resources is often made up for by keen pupils and enthusiastic teachers.

FALKIRK COUNCIL
LIBRARY SUPPORT
FOR SCHOOLS

Glossary

accounting technician trainee accountant

algebra type of maths in which letters and symbols are used to represent quantities

analyse to study something in detail in order to understand it

analytical using a logical method of thinking about something in order to understand it

antivirus software computer programs that protect your computer against viruses that can damage it

automate to make something work by machinery

bank organisation that provides financial services, such as lending money

building society organisation like a bank that provides financial services, especially loans to buy houses and other buildings

bursar person who looks after the finances of a college or university

code system of numbers, words, letters or symbols used to represent information or keep it secret

data facts or information; also means information stored by a computer

economy production, supply and trade in a particular place or country

encode to change information into code

financial record report about the financial activities of a business, person, or other group

forecast to predict what will happen in the future

ICT Information and Communications Technology

insurance when someone pays money regularly to a company that agrees to pay them money back, for example if they are injured or lose something

interest fixed charge added to what someone has borrowed; or extra amount added to what someone has saved

IT Information Technology

less developed countries countries without major industries and in which most people earn a low income

logically based on reason and facts

logistics planning and organisation needed to make a scheme or a company work

operational researcher person who analyses complex problems mathematically to work out solutions

pension regular payment to someone (usually aged over 60) that allows them to live without working

phishing to send emails under a false name in order to acquire confidential information such as passwords or bank details

profit financial benefit

program sequence of instructions for a computer

salary fixed amount of money paid to somebody for the work that they do

shares units of equal value into which a company is divided and sold in order to raise money; people who own shares receive part of the company's profits

tax money that people have to pay a government so that it can pay for public services

Further information

There are many courses, apprenticeships and jobs using mathematics, so where do you go to find out more? It is really useful to meet up with careers advisers at school or college and to attend careers fairs to see the range of opportunities available. Remember that public libraries and newspapers are other important sources of information. The earlier you check out your options, the better prepared you will be to put your maths skills to good use as you earn a living in future.

Books

Math (Discovering Careers for Your Future) Ferguson Publishing, Facts On File Inc, 2008

Career Ideas for Kids Who Like Math and Money (Career Ideas for Kids), Diane Lindsey Reeves and Lindsey Clasen, Facts On File Inc, 2007

What Next After School?: All You Need to Know About Work, Travel and Study, Elizabeth Holmes, Kogan Page, 2010

Websites

www.mathscareers.org.uk/ This website tells you about famous mathematicians and the ways they have solved problems, and describes a range of maths-related jobs.

www.prospects.ac.uk/options_ mathematics_your_skills.htm
Aimed at maths graduates, this website gives a clear idea of what routes to take for maths careers, and includes a comprehensive list of resources and contacts.

www.plus.maths.org/content/Career
An online maths magazine that contains interviews with people who took maths-related degree courses.

www.mathscareers.org.uk/16-19/ career_profiles.cfm
A website containing maths-related career profiles.

www.futuremorph.org/ scienceandmaths/#/intro
An interactive website that gives lots of suggestions for where maths and science studies can take you. It also gives you an idea of the earning and travel potential of some careers.

www.brightknowledge.org/ brightknowledge-scheme/resources/ knowledge-bank/science-and-maths/ careers-in-science-and-maths
A variety of people with jobs in maths and science explain what their careers involve.

Index

I'M GOOD AT...

Contents of all the titles in the series:

WAYLAND